文化之旅

同济大学（四平路校区）

CULTURAL JOURNEY OF TONGJI UNIVERSITY (SIPING ROAD CAMPUS)

周宏武 主编

同济大学出版社
Tongji University Press

图书在版编目(CIP)数据

同济大学文化之旅:四平路校区/周宏武主编. --
上海:同济大学出版社,2019.3
ISBN 978-7-5608-8388-5

Ⅰ.①同… Ⅱ.①周… Ⅲ.①同济大学-校园文化-
介绍 Ⅳ.① G649.285.1

中国版本图书馆 CIP 数据核字(2019)第 005717 号

同济大学文化之旅(四平路校区)
周宏武 主编

出 品 人	华春荣	
责任编辑	陆克 丽霞	
责任校对	徐春莲	
出版发行	同济大学出版社 www.tongjipress.com.cn	
	(地址:上海市四平路 1239 号 邮编:200092 电话:021-65985622)	
经 销	全国各地新华书店	
印 刷	上海安枫印务有限公司	
开 本	787mm×1092mm 1/32	
印 张	2.875	
字 数	64000	
版 次	2019 年 3 月第 1 版 2019 年 3 月第 1 次印刷	
书 号	ISBN 978-7-5608-8388-5	
定 价	36.00 元	

版权所有 侵权必究 印刷问题 负责调换

主 编
周宏武

副主编
周春玲　喻　娟

摄 影
姜锡祥　江　平

翻 译
李　梅

建筑素描
孙彤宇

地图绘画
周叶渊　张康硕　朱礼才淇

前　言

历史长河，浩瀚奔涌；百年学府，巍巍上庠。

大学孕育了文化，文化滋养着大学。文化是大学最显著的特质，是一所大学的软实力，拥有精神高地和文化底蕴，是中国特色、世界一流大学建设的前提、基础和必然要求。

同济大学创建于 1907 年，110 余年来，其志不渝，始终与中华民族休戚与共、与祖国科教事业心手相连、与上海城市发展相濡以沫。同济大学在办学过程中，形成了独有的文化特质，"同舟共济"的校训，"与祖国同行，以科教济世"的使命担当，"同心同德同舟楫，济人济事济天下"的家国情怀，"同济天下"的大学理想……这一切，早已深深地铭刻在大学发展的印迹之中。

同济大学高度重视大学文化建设，始终以传承人类文明、振兴民族文化、弘扬大学精神为己任，积极培育和践行社会主义核心价值观，不断完善由"文化导向引领""文化环境培育""文化载体支撑"和"文化影响传播"四大平台构筑的、具有同济特色的大学文化格局。以文化人，以德润心。学校进一步完善和优化了大学文化软硬件环境，着力推进文化有形载体建设，通过优化、美化环境助推环境育人；注重构建公共文化平台，不断丰富校园文艺生活；注重学院学科文化建设，形成"各美其美，美美与共"的校园文化生态，进一步发挥大学文化的情感浸润功能，增强师生的文化自信和文化自觉。

大学校园不仅是求知的场所，更是陶冶情操、守护心灵的净土。大学的校园景观积淀着历史、传统、文化和社会的价值，同时蕴含着巨大的潜在教育意义。为深入发掘同济校园特色文化资源，展现深厚的校园环境文化底蕴，打造适合师生、校友、来访者实地体验的参观访学路线，推广同济品牌文化，《同济大学文化之旅》（四平路校区）应运而生。本书推出同济大学四平路校区的"紫色建筑之路""红色人文之路""绿色节能之路""蓝色科技之路"四条线路，以图文并茂的形式和各具特色的视角介绍了四平路校区的文化景观和平台。

一书一世界，一卷一洞天。徜徉在风景如画的同济校园里，欣赏着一草一木、一花一石，观察着细微的景观、独特的建筑，感受着文字表达与实景画面的交互印证，体会着审美情趣和价值追求的深厚蕴含，相信每一位参观者都会被这些文化景观所渗透出来的精神品质和文化气质深深感染，不知不觉融入到这赏心悦目的情境之中。

编者

Preface

The long river of time rushes forward boundlessly; a century-old educational establishment is great, indeed.

A university creates its own culture, which in turn nourishes the university. The culture represents the soft power of the university; therefore, it is necessary to explore the rich cultural resources in building a world-class university with Chinese characteristics.

Founded in 1907, Tongji University has been dedicated to the Chinese nation, to the cause of science and education in China, and to the local development of Shanghai during its 110 years of history. Over the years, Tongji University has developed a unique culture which is reflected in its motto of "striving together on the same boat", its mission of "developing together with the country and benefiting the world with science and technology", and its aspirations of "serving the people, the cause and the world with one heart and on the same boat". All this has been deeply imprinted in the development of the university.

The University has been active in promoting the core values of socialism by inheriting human civilization, revitalizing the national culture, and enhancing the university spirit. Tongji has constantly improved its four platforms of "cultural orientation" "cultural environment" "cultural support" and "cultural communication" for establishment of the university culture framework with Tongji characteristics. To nourish people of Tongji with culture, and to nurture their heart with virtues, the university has further optimized the university cultural environment, both physical and spiritual, to promote the construction of tangible cultural media in recent years. It endeavors to enhance the cultivation of people through optimizing the cultural environment, to construct the culture platforms through enriching the campus life, to improve academic disciplinary culture through forming the campus cultural ecology of "coexistence of individual and collective beauty", and to strengthen the cultural confidence as well as cultural consciousness in teachers and students through infiltrating the university culture.

The university campus is not only a place for pursuit of knowledge, but also a land for extolling the virtues of the mankind. The landscape at the university campuses is imbedded with the history, traditions, cultures and values of the university, which is of potential educational significance. *Cultural Journey of Tongji University (Siping Road Campus)* was compiled to explore the unique cultural resources at Tongji campuses for a better understanding of its profound campus culture and promotion of Tongji brand culture in addition to designing a sightseeing route suitable for the teachers, students, Tongji alumni and its visitors. The book focuses on four paths at the Siping campus, i.e. the Purple Path of Buildings of Distinctive Styles, the Red Path of Building and Places of Humanistic Features, the Green Path of Buildings of Energy Conservation and the Blue Path of Buildings of Science and Technology. Cultural attractions and platforms are presented in both words and pictures from distinctive perspectives in the book.

One may see the world from a book and the sky from a painting. Readers may feel the interaction between words and pictures, experience the aesthetic taste, and appreciate the profound cultural values by wandering in the picturesque Tongji campus, enjoying the plants, flowers and stones, and observing the unique landscape and architecture. It is hoped that visitors will be impressed by the spiritual and cultural qualities and immersed unconsciously with the pleasing environment.

The Editor

同济大学简介

同济大学历史悠久、声誉卓著，是教育部直属并与上海市共建的全国重点大学。经过110余年的发展，同济大学已经成为一所特色鲜明，具有国际影响力的综合性、研究型、国际化大学。学校入选世界一流大学建设A类高校，正向着"扎根中国大地建设世界一流大学"目标愿景阔步迈进。

同济大学设有29个学院，7家附属医院，6所附属中小学。有四平路、嘉定、沪西、沪北4个校区，占地面积2.54平方公里，校舍总建筑面积180余万平方米，图书馆总藏书量445万余册。

学校现有全日制本科生17 757人，硕士研究生12 852人，博士研究生5 246人。另有外国留学生3 468人。拥有专任教师2 814人，其中专业技术职务正高级1 028人，中国科学院院士10人（含双聘），中国工程院院士13人（含双聘），第三世界科学院院士2人，美国工程院外籍院士1人，瑞典皇家工程科学院外籍院士1人，德国工程院外籍院士1人，比利时皇家科学与艺术学院外籍院士1人。国家"千人计划"学者42人，教育部"长江计划"特聘（讲座）教授35人，国家重点基础研究发展计划首席科学家23人，国家重点研发计划首席科学家35人，国家杰出青年科学基金获得者50人，国家级教学名师4人。国家自然科学基金创新群体8个，教育部创新团队9个，国家级教学团队6个。

学校学科设置涵盖工学、理学、医学、管理学、经济学、哲学、文学、法学、教育学、艺术学10个门类。现有本科招生专业85个（其中50个专业按17个专业大类招生），硕士学位一级学科授权点47个，专业硕士学位授权点18个，博士学位授权学科点涵盖一级学科31个，专业博士学位授权点3个，博士后流动站25个。其中，国家一级重点学科3个，国家二级重点学科（含培育）10个，上海高校一流学科17个。拥有3个国家重点实验室、1个国家工程实验室、1个国家协同创新中心、1个国家大型科学仪器中心、5个国家工程（技术）研究中心以及53个省部级重点实验室和工程（技术）研究中心。

（统计数据截至2018年9月）

Introduction

Tongji University, is a venerable and prestigious institution of higher education which is directly under the Ministry of Education and cobuilt by Shanghai Municipality. After more than 110 years of development, Tongji University has become a comprehensive and research-oriented university with distinctive features and international fame. Tongji University selected as one of the Class A universities in the World-leading University Construction program of China, it is currently working towards accomplishing the mission of a China based world-class university.

Tongji University has set up 29 schools, 7 affiliated hospitals and 6 affiliated primary and secondary schools. It has four campuses, namely Siping, Jiading, Huxi and Hubei, covering an area of 2.54 square kilometers of which the building coverage is about 1.8 million square meters. The university library has 4.45 million books.

Tongji university has 17,757 full-time registered undergraduates, 12,852 registered master students, 5,246 registered Ph. D students and 3,468 international students. Our university has 2,814 faculty members, of whom there are 1,028 professors, 10 members of Chinese Academy of Sciences, 13 members of Chinese Academy of Engineering, two members of the Academy of Sciences for the Developing World, a foreign associate of US National Academy of Engineering and a foreign member of Royal Swedish Academy of Engineering Sciences, a foreign member of German Academy of Science and Engineering, and an international member of the Royal Academies for Science and the Arts of Belgium. Besides, there are 42 scholars listed in the national Recruitment Program of Global Experts, 35 professors of Changjiang Scholars Program by the Ministry of Education, 23 chief scientists of National Basic Research Program of China, 35 chief scientists of National Major Research Program of China, 50 professors of National Outstanding Young Scholars Program and 4 national level teachers with excellent teaching quality. Our university has also established 8 innovation communities of Natural Science Foundation of China, 9 innovation communities directly under the Ministry of Education and 6 national-level teaching teams.

Tongji University covers 10 categories of academic disciplines, including, engineering, science, medicine, management, economics, philosophy, humanities, law, education and arts. It has 85 undergraduate majors, of which 50 majors enroll students under 17 broad disciplinary categories. It has 47 programs authorized to confer academic master degree, 18 programs to confer professional master degree. With regard to Ph.D programs, Tongji University has 31 programs authorized to confer academic doctoral degree, 3 programs to confer professional doctoral degree and 25 postdoctoral research stations.

Among all the disciplines, there are 3 first-level national key disciplines, 10 second level national key disciplines and 17 first-level Shanghai disciplines. Tongji University is also equipped with 3 state key laboratories, 1 national engineering laboratory, 1 national collaborative innovation center, 1 national large-scale instrument center, 5 national engineering (technology) research centers and 53 ministerial provincial-level key labs and engineering (technology) research centers.

(Date updated by September 2018)

目 录
Table of Content

Cultural Journey of Tongji University

2 紫色之路（建筑类）

图书馆、南北教学楼、衷和楼（教学科研综合楼）、建筑与城市规划学院C楼、文远楼、瑞安楼、大礼堂、土木工程学院、一·二九礼堂、中法中心、逸夫楼

24 红色之路（人文景观类）

四平路校区正门、毛主席塑像、国立柱、闻学堂、校史馆、国豪园、三好坞、孔园（千秋园）、爱校路（樱花大道）、德文图书馆、一·二九纪念园、博物馆、旭日楼（校友之家）、师魂石碑

48 绿色之路（节能类）

行政楼、文远楼、运筹楼、人工湿地、学生浴室、大礼堂、环境科学与工程学院实验楼、游泳馆、中法中心、上海国际设计一场

62 蓝色之路（科技类）

建筑与城市规划学院艺术造型实验室、声学馆、物理实践工作站、结构试验中心、土木工程教学创新实践基地、同济创业谷、深海探索馆、同济大学Fablab、微小飞机实验室

2   The Purple Path – Buildings of Distinctive Styles

The University Library, The South and North Teaching Buildings, Zhonghe Building (comprehensive building for teaching and research), Building C of the College of Architecture and Urban Planning, Wenyuan Building, Rui'an Building, The Auditorium, College of Civil Engineering, The 1·29 Auditorium, The Sino-French Center, Yifu Building

24   The Red Path – Building and Places of Humanistic Features

The main entrance of the Siping Campus, The Statue of Chairman Mao, The Memorial Columns, Haven of Classical Literature, The University History Gallery, Guohao Park, Sanhaowu Garden, Kongyuan Garden (Qianqiu Garden), Aixiao Road (the Sakura Avenue), German Library, The 1·29 Memorial Park, The University Museum, Xuri Building (Alumni's Home), The Shihun (Teacher's Soul) Stelae

48   The Green Path - Buildings of Energy Conservation

The Administration Building, Wenyuan Building, Yunchou Building, The Artificial Wetland, The Student Shower House, The Auditorium, Environmental Engineering Center, The Swimming Pool, Sino-French Center, Shanghai International Design Center

62   The Blue Path – Buildings of Science and Technology

The Innovation Laboratory of College of Architectural Design and Urban Planning, The Institute of Acoustics, The Physical Experiment Workstation, The Structure Testing Center, The Civil Engineering Innovation Teaching Base, Venture Valley of Tongji University, The Deep Sea Exploration Gallery, The Creative Workshop of College of Design and Innovation, The Simulation Plane Workstation

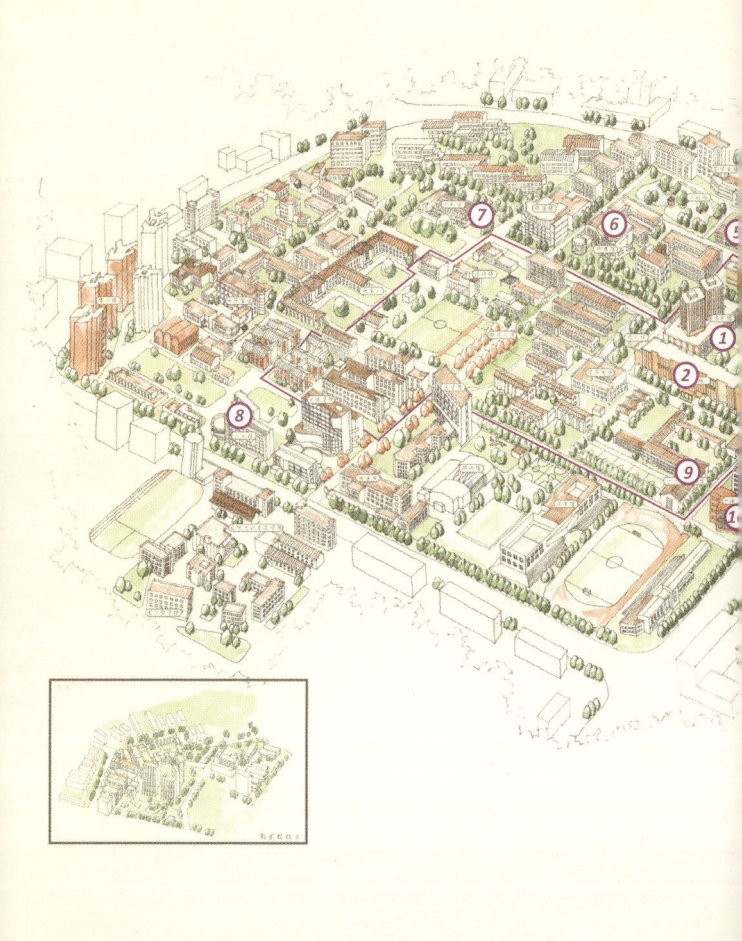

紫色之路（建筑类）
The Purple Path
Buildings of Distinctive Styles

○ 1 图书馆
   2 南北教学楼
   3 衷和楼
     （教学科研综合楼）
   4 建筑与城市规划学院C楼
   5 文远楼
   6 瑞安楼
   7 大礼堂
   8 土木工程学院
   9 一·二九礼堂
  10 中法中心
  11 逸夫楼

○ 1. The University Library
2. The South and North Teaching Buildings
3. Zhonghe Building (comprehensive building for teaching and research)
4. Building C of the College of Architecture and Urban Planning
5. Wenyuan Building
6. Rui'an Building
7. The Auditorium
8. College of Civil Engineering
9. The 1·29 Auditorium
10. The Sino-French Center
11. Yifu Building

1 图书馆
The University Library

走进同济大学四平路校门,在校园的中轴线上,毛主席像的正后方,两座十一层塔楼仿佛悬在空中,远远看去,像一本打开的书。这就是四平路校区图书馆。

图书馆始建于二十世纪六十年代中期,属二层框架结构内院式布置。后历经多次改建,二十世纪八十年代中期的扩建工程中,在内院凌空架起塔楼,外墙采用清水红砖,间以白色线条,处理简洁、明快,富含中国传统建筑的神韵。2003年改建后,最大限度增加了阅览活动空间,开放院落空间与校园环境相融合,同时整合不同年代的建筑特色,以透明形态的轻度介入,激发整体建筑的活力。位于图书馆南10楼的闻学堂于2013年开放,集传统文献借阅、展示、研讨等功能于一体,是学校重要的中华传统文化传承基地。

图书馆拥有丰富的馆藏量。印刷型资源有图书317万多册、中文现刊2 495种、外文现刊840种、期刊合订本17万册;另外,电子资源包括电子图书100万多册,数据库54种,其中电子中文期刊12 649种,电子外文期刊17 463种。

Upon entering the main entrance of the Siping Campus, you will see the Statue of Chairman Mao right in front of you. Beyond the statue, there stand on the central axis of the campus two 11-storey elevated tower buildings in the shape of an opened book. This is the University Library on the Siping Campus.

Built in the mid-1960s, the Library had a two-story inner frame structure in the style of a courtyard. After a series of adaptations, the twin towers rose from inside the old frame structure following an expansion in the 1980s. The walls of the two-story outer parts of the Library were decorated with plain red bricks lined with white cement for the joints. This simple yet elegant style showcased the charm of traditional Chinese architecture. The restructure of the Library in 2003 expanded the reading space to the greatest extent. The brick walls of the courtyard were partially replaced with light and transparent wall glasses for the inner open space to integrate with its surrounding environment. In this way, the library which has drawn on styles of different ages is enriched with architectural vitality. The Haven of Classical Literature was set up on the 10th floor of the library in 2013. People can read, attend exhibitions, and hold seminars on Chinese culture. It has become an important base to inherit and promote traditional Chinese culture.

The rich collections of the Library include more than 3,170,000 printed books, 2,495 kinds of journals in Chinese, 840 kinds of international journals, 170,000 bound volumes of journals. In addition, e-resources of the Library consist of 1,000,000 e-books, 54 databases which include 12,649 electronic Chinese and 17,463 electronic international journals.

2 南北教学楼
The South and North Teaching Buildings

在图书馆的南北两侧，对称分布着两栋砌体结构、比例考究、细节精美的四层大楼，平面呈一字形，与图书馆大楼一同围合出一片庄重而祥和的空间。

南北教学楼作为同济大学的主要教学楼，分别建于1953年和1954年。原来的设计平面采用轴线对称式，立面造型采用中国传统的大屋顶式样，并有汉白玉栏杆、立面雕花和梁栋彩画等装饰。后为了适应崇尚节俭的时代精神，教学楼改为平屋顶，局部作挑檐处理，上部为砖砌镂空女儿墙，建筑底层以水泥粉刷成仿虚弥座式的基座，外墙为当时流行的清水红砖墙。

南北教学楼是一组凝结了同济记忆的经典建筑，一代又一代的同济人在这里留下了难忘的回忆。2005年，南北楼被列入上海市第四批优秀历史建筑保护名单。

南北教学楼绿树红墙交相辉映，构成了校园里一道亮丽的景观。北楼北侧的香樟园和南楼西首的问源园都是晨读的好去处。

On both the south and north sides of the University Library lie symmetrically two four-story red brick teaching buildings with well-designed proportion and exquisite details. The two buildings with a straight-line layout echoes with the Library to produce a solemnly peaceful area on campus.

The South and North Teaching Buildings built in 1953 and 1954 have functioned as the main teaching buildings on the Siping Campus since then. They were originally designed symmetrically with Chinese traditional big roofs and white marble handrails, and decorated with carvings and painting on the beams. To pursue a life style of simplicity which was popular at the time, the buildings were eventually completed with terrace roofs, overhanging eaves and brick tracery parapets. For the base of the buildings, cement dressing was used for an effect of sumeru style, and the then popular plain red bricks were chosen for the outer walls.

The Teaching Buildings have witnessed the development of Tongji University for over half a century, and are regarded as classical buildings at Tongji. Generations of teachers and students have had their unforgettable memories related to the two buildings. In 2005, the South and North Teaching Buildings were included in the fourth group of Outstanding Historical Building Protection list of Shanghai.

The verdant and luxuriant trees and bushes around the buildings echo with the red bricks of the buildings to create a charming view of life. The Xiangzhang Garden on the north side of the North Teaching Building and Wenyuan Garden to the west of the South Teaching Building provide perfect places for students to do their morning reading.

3 衷和楼（教学科研综合楼）
Zhonghe Building (comprehensive building for teaching and research)

位于同济大学四平路校区东北角的衷和楼，建成于 2007 年，是百年校庆的标志性建筑。大楼地上 21 层，象征二十一世纪；高度约 100 米，意蕴建校一百周年。

大楼建筑外形像叠加起来的"巨型魔方"，建筑为近 50 米的正方形柱体，呈 7 个三层高的 L 形单元，这些单元沿竖向顺时针 90 度螺旋上升，勾勒出虚实相间的外部形态，极具时代感。内部大空间、"楼中楼"的独特布局凸显出别具一格的现代设计理念，大空间的楼层中分别设置了不同类型阶梯教室、球形多媒体会议中心、会议厅、咖啡厅等 9 座风格各异的"楼中楼"。大楼的中央大厅，呈 16 米 ×16 米见方空间从地面直接贯空近百米高的楼顶，是目前国内高层建筑中少见的结构形式。

Zhonghe Building was built in 2007 at the northeast corner of the Siping Campus as a landmark for Tongji's centennial anniversary. Its 21 storeys represent the 21st century, and its height of 100 meters symbolize the university's centennial anniversary.

From a distance, Zhonghe Building looks like a stack of Rubik's cubes which turn out to be a fifty-meter-tall big square cube made up of seven L-shaped units of three-floors in height. These units spiral up clockwise at an angel of 90°, projecting a space intervened with intangibility and reality and painting a strong sense of the contemporary time. Contemporary architectural concepts of large space and "building inside a building" were employed for the interior design of the building. Inside the building there are nine large space buildings of different styles such as lecture theaters, a spheroidal multimedia conference center, conference halls, and a cafe. Among them, the most impressive structure is the central hall. It is 16m×16m in space, and 100m in height, stretching right from the 1st floor to the top of the building, a rare structural design for high-rise buildings in China.

4 建筑与城市规划学院 C 楼
Building C of the College of Architecture and Urban Planning

建成于 2004 年的建筑与城市规划学院 C 楼，地下 1 层，地上 7 层。主要用于科研和研究生教学。

C 楼的风格独特，其核心是居中贯穿东西的连廊系统，包括贯穿二至七层所有工作楼面的直跑景观楼梯，以及一系列上下贯通的光井，充足的天光和连续弥漫的空间使它成为师生的交往场所。北侧的连续叠加的室内下沉榕树园，三层的竹园，以及屋顶室外榉树园，虚实套叠，丰富了内部空间。大楼注重功能模块化，不同的空间类型在立面的形式、质感上得到了清晰的区分。地下室提供了展厅及绿化中庭，建筑南侧架空部分引入叠水及阶梯式花圃，学生制作的小木桥横卧水面，使其生机盎然。

建筑师：张斌、周蔚。

Building C of the College of Architecture and Urban Planning, Tongji University was built in 2004. With seven storeys and a basement, it is mainly used for research and teaching of graduate students.

Building C is characterized by its particular architectural style. A central long-span corridor runs from the east to the west inside the building, connecting the sightseeing staircases from the second floor all the way to the seventh floor. There are a series of vertical light wells linking the ground floor with the top one. The large space with natural lighting provides ideal places for communication among teachers and students. In the north part of the building, there are three overlapping indoor gardens: a sunken banyan garden, a three-story bamboo garden, and a rooftop zelkova garden. They not only enrich the interior space, but also function as filters of the buildings to the environment. In addition, different spaces for various functions inside the building are materialized in distinctive forms. There is an exhibition hall and a green area in the basement. In the elevated part to the south of the building, water runs down stepped flower beds to a small pond where lies a wooden bridge made by students.

Architects: ZHANG Bin, ZHOU Wei.

5 文远楼
Wenyuan Building

北大道的绿树浓荫中,掩映着一座淡灰色的老建筑,简洁典雅,其风格跟周围的建筑有明显的区别,这就是著名的文远楼。而在建筑界内,同济大学文远楼更是被奉为经典之作,入选《世界建筑史》和《中国建筑史》。

1993年获中国建筑学会"优秀建筑创作奖",1999年获"新中国50年上海经典建筑"铜奖。2004年,包括文远楼在内的同济大学历史建筑群成为上海市第四批优秀历史建筑。

文远楼建造于1954年,是典型的三层不对称的错层式、钢筋混凝土框架结构建筑。这幢建筑从平面布局到立面处理,从空间组织到结构形式都大胆而成功地运用了现代建筑的观念和手法,是我国最早的典型的包豪斯风格的建筑。

走进文远楼,不论是进厅、房间还是楼梯,不论是空间的布局,功能的处理还是构件、细节的设计,都体现了设计者独到的现代建筑理念。没有一处多余的空间,每个空间都有其自身存在的必要。

建筑师:黄毓麟、哈雄文。

结构师:俞载道。

Amid the green trees and bushes beyond the North Road lies an old gray building which stands out among the surrounding ones for its simplicity and elegance. This is Wenyuan Building, well-known as a classical masterpiece in the field of architecture and has been listed in both History of World Architecture and History of Chinese Architecture for decades. The design of the building won an Outstanding Architectural Innovation Award issued by the Architectural Society of China in 1993, and a bronze prize in the selection of the Shanghai Classical Architecture for New China's 50th Anniversary in 1999. In 2004, Wenyuan Building was included on the list of 4th Group of Architectural Heritage of Shanghai Municipal Government among a group of historic buildings of Tongji.

Wenyuan Building, built in 1954, is a typical three-story, asymmetric, split-level architecture in reinforced concrete frame structure. Modern architectural ideas and techniques were boldly and successfully employed in its layout, elevations, space arrangement and overall structure so that people would naturally associate the image of the building with Bauhaus.

Inside the building, one would also find in its reception hall, rooms, and stairs the manifestation of the designers' modern architectural ideas in the space arrangement, functional layout and detailed design -- there is no redundant space, and each part of the overall space has a purpose.

Architects: HUANG Yulin, HA Xiongwen.
Structural Engineer: YU Zaidao.

6 瑞安楼
Rui'an Building

瑞安楼主要入口朝南。简洁明快的造型,腾飞向上的形象,纯洁素雅的色彩,虚实互补的立面,给人以清新的感觉。金属外壳的屋顶象一个巨型的银梭,平添了建筑的动感。

内部平面布局分为南北两部分。内部中庭空间设计是本建筑的最大特色,可以用作展览、庆典、集会等,是多功能的交流场所。中庭东端的观光电梯拉开了空间的纵深感,更增添了一份活力。

瑞安楼竣工于 2000 年,主体 8 层,由香港瑞安集团董事局主席、上海荣誉市民罗康瑞先生捐资修建,是全国首座落成的研究生专用教学设施。

建筑师:戴复东、吴庐生。

The main entrance of Rui'an Building faces the South Entrance of the Siping Campus. The building greets people with a refreshing image by a combination of its simple design, soaring pose, elegant colors and complementary elevations. The metallic roof bears a resemblance to a huge silver shuttle, bringing dynamics to the building.

The indoor layout characterized by a spacious central hall is composed of two parts of south and north. This special hall is multifunctional for exhibitions, ceremonial events and meetings. The sightseeing elevator at the east end of the hall elaborates the imposing height of the hall and the dynamic feature of the inner space.

The eight-storey building, completed in 2000, was funded by Mr. Lo Hong-shui, chairman of Hong Kong-based Shui On Group and a Honorary Citizen of Shanghai. It was the first building constructed exclusively for teaching graduate students in China.

Architects: DAI Fudong, WU Lusheng.

7 大礼堂
The Auditorium

曾被誉为"亚洲第一跨"的大礼堂,建成于1962年,是同济现代主义建筑的代表之作。1999年被提名为"新中国50年上海经典建筑"。

大礼堂所采用的钢筋混凝土预应力联方网架、双曲薄壳屋面结构,屋顶仅厚5厘米。虽然体量和容量十分庞大,而礼堂内部却没有一根柱子,拱形结构自身又赋予建筑真实而独具特色的形式,给人以简洁、轻盈的视觉感受。2005年,大礼堂进行了保护性修缮改造。重点保护礼堂拱形网壳结构,屋面由油毡板制成网格单元,室内屋顶采用结构露明的做法,表现了纯粹的结构形态,展示了其韵律美。大礼堂每年举办30余场各种大型文艺活动,是学校重要的文化活动场所。

建筑师:黄家骅、胡纫茉。
结构师:俞载道、冯之椿。

The Auditorium, built in 1962 and hailed as the No. 1 long span Auditorium in Asia for years, is very representative of Tongji's modern architecture. In 1999, it was nominated in the selection of the Shanghai Classical Architecture for New China's 50th Anniversary.

The Auditorium was constructed with reinforced concrete, pre-stressed grid structure and hyperbolic thin roof at the thickness of just 5cm. Despite its large space and capacity, the Auditorium does not have any load bearing pillars inside. In addition, the smooth and light arch roof brings visual pleasure in that it adds elegant gracefulness to the Auditorium. The Auditorium underwent a renovation for protective purposes in 2005. The outer wall was reconstructed with linoleum grid, and the ceiling with exposed skeleton to support the arch structure and to explicitly display its structure with rhythmic beauty. Every year, more than 30 important activities are held in the Auditorium which serves as a major venue for cultural activities at the university.

Architects: HUANG Jiahua, HU Renmo.
Structural Engineers: YU Zaidao, FENG Zhichun.

8 土木工程学院
College of Civil Engineering

土木工程学院大楼建成于2004年,地上8层,地下1层。

整个大楼采用全钢结构形式,外墙采用相配合的挂板,整体体现出现代建筑结构的优越性,是一个成功的钢结构建筑的教学案例,为同济大学校园内第一幢真正意义上的钢结构建筑物。

建筑主副楼之间以一定的角度布置,使整体形象打破了板式建筑的单调感,更重要的是通过体量的倾斜与重组,建筑体之间的组合关系达到了和谐,功能与形态之间也取得了统一。大楼整体上采用全钢结构式的外露设计模式,在增加其浓厚现代气息的同时,也符合了现代教学示范的要求,充分提供了教学与参观的平台。

建筑师:钱锋。

The building of the College of Civil Engineering was completed in 2004 with eight floors above the ground and one floor under the ground.

The building was constructed with full-steel structure and matching cladding for its exterior walls, which was a proud demonstration of the superiority of advanced modern structures. It has become not only an excellent instance of steel-structure construction, but also the first genuine architecture of steel structures at Tongji University.

The harmonious spatial arrangement between the main and the annex buildings not only avoids the architectural monotony of slab-structure buildings, but also combines its functions with its physical forms. The exposure of steel structures was designed to enhance its modern features of the building and to facilitate teaching of civil engineering students.

Architect: QIAN Feng.

9 一·二九礼堂
The 1·29 Auditorium

一·二九礼堂始建于 1942 年，后来为纪念同济大学 1948 年 1 月 29 日学生爱国运动而得名。

2001 年，以尊重校园历史、保护校园环境的理念对其进行改建，将历史建筑的保留部分作为新建筑的一个组成部分，表现出自身的建筑美感和历史价值。北部加建了钢和玻璃的入口大堂，恢复原山墙柱廊式结构；门廊的细圆柱意在与对面羽毛球馆门廊的混凝土柱形成对话，并通过二者之间的纪念园入口空地形成对景；原来的外立面通过修葺成为改建后的内立面，钢木屋架暴露、墙面的处理等内部改造手法都能在满足特殊功能要求的同时，创造一种舒适的美感。

The 1·29 Auditorium was built in 1942 which was named after the patriotic movement initiated by Tongji students in Jan. 29th, 1948.

In 2001, the Auditorium underwent a renovation under the principle of respecting the history while protecting the environment. The preserved part of the historic building became part the new Auditorium to show its architectural aesthetics and historic values. An entrance made of steel and armored glass was added to the northern part of the building; and the original gable colonnades were restored. The slim columns on the porch of the 1·29 Auditorium started a conversation with the reinforced concrete columns on the porch of the badminton gym opposite the Auditorium and formed a mirrored scenery with the space at the entrance of the 1·29 Memorial Park between the two buildings. The exterior walls were turned into interior ones after the renovation; and the exposed steel structures and renovated inner walls both satisfied special architectural needs and created delightful aesthetic pleasure.

10 中法中心
The Sino-French Center

在一·二九礼堂的东面,有一座由锈红色体块的大斜坡与白色体块穿插组成的醒目建筑——中法中心。锈红色体块与白色体块都往北部延伸至二者叠合,两个体块是一种并置的关系,形成了"双手相握"的造型;而二者之间又相对独立、造型不同却又逐渐走向融合,展现了"和而不同"的内涵。整个建筑旨在体现中法两国的文化差异与和谐共存。

中法中心2004年始建,于2006年建成。地上5层,地下1层。

建筑师:张斌、周蔚。

To the east of The 1·29 Auditorium lies a striking building made of a rusty slope and a white cube. This is the Sino-French Center. The rusty slope block and the white cube block extend to the north till they meet and overlap. On the one hand, the two blocks are juxtaposed to form an image of "shaking hands"; on the other hand, the two blocks are independent with distinctive designs. The design conveys a traditional Chinese philosophical idea -- harmony in diversity. The building symbolizes the harmonious existence with different cultures between China and France.

The construction of the Sino-French Center with five above-ground floors and one underground floor started in 2004 and completed in 2006.

Architects: ZHANG Bin, ZHOU Wei.

11 逸夫楼
Yifu Building

逸夫楼坐落在四平路校门的南侧,外观极富时代感和雕塑感,简练的流线外观配以局部的半圆、圆、球体造型,墙角及大面积玻璃窗转角大都采用了圆弧,使厚实的大

块体量柔和了许多。建筑设计上,既强调个性,又注重与环境的协调,建筑形态简洁又富于变化,细部的处理和色彩的运用,营造了一种既现代又典雅、既庄重又亲切的氛围,各种功能、空间的关系处理得有理、有序,让人感觉美好、难忘。

逸夫楼由香港邵逸夫先生赠款,国家教委与同济大学共同投资兴建,1993年年底竣工。曾获邵逸夫先生第五批大陆赠款项目工程一等奖第一名,1994年度上海市建筑工程"白玉兰"奖,国家教委优秀设计项目一等奖,城乡建设部优秀建筑设计评选获奖项目一等奖,全国第七届优秀工程设计项目银质奖。

建筑师:戴复东、吴庐生。

Yifu Building lies to the south of the main entrance of the Siping Campus. Its modern, sculptural look is attributable to its simple and straight-line design coupled with circular, semicircular, and spherical shapes. The curved designs for corners and large glass windows adds tenderness to the building blocks. The architectural design highlights both the uniqueness of the building and its adaptation with the surrounding environment. Its simple outlook with rich details and colors creates a modern and elegant, majestic and friendly atmosphere in the building. Inside the building, different functions are reasonably arranged in proper spaces, making the venue a place hard to forget.

Yifu Building, completed in 1993, was funded by Mr. SHAW Yifu from Hong Kong with joint investment by the State Education Commission and Tongji University. It has won a number of prizes including the first place of the First Prize on SHAW's 5th donation list for projects in Chinese mainland, a Magnolia Prize for Shanghai Construction Projects 1994, a first prize of Outstanding Architectural Designs by the State Education Commission, and a first prize of Outstanding Architectural Designs by the Ministry of Housing and Urban-Rural Development, and a silver medal in the 7th National Excellent Design Projects.

Architects: DAI Fudong, WU Lusheng.

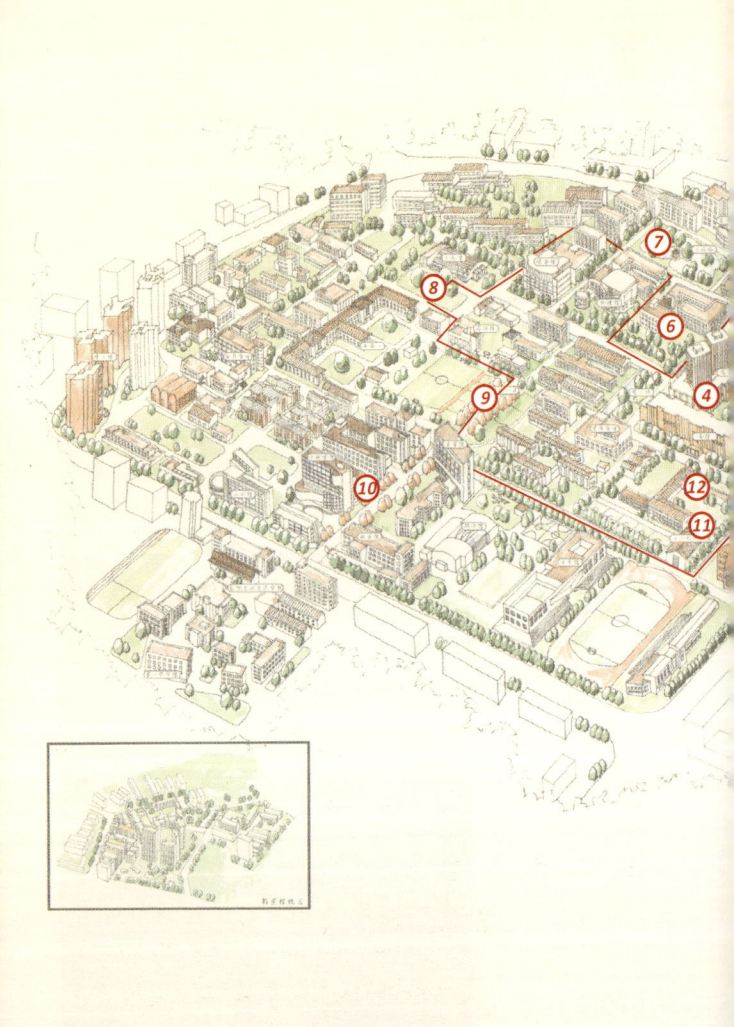

红色之路 (人文景观类)
The Red Path
Building and Places of Humanistic Features

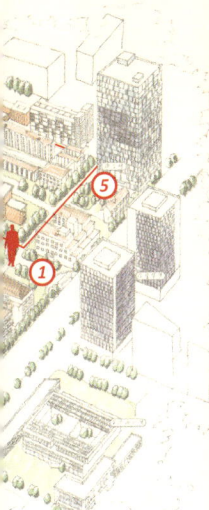

○ 1 四平路校区正门	○ 1. The main entrance of the Siping Campus
2 毛主席塑像	2. The Statue of Chairman Mao
3 国立柱	3. The Memorial Columns
4 闻学堂	4. Haven of Classical Literature
5 校史馆	5. The University History Gallery
6 国豪园	6. Guohao Park
7 三好坞	7. Sanhaowu Garden
8 孔园(千秋园)	8. Kongyuan Garden (Qianqiu Garden)
9 爱校路(樱花大道)	9. Aixiao Road (the Sakura Avenue)
10 德文图书馆	10. German Library
11 一·二九纪念园	11. The 1·29 Memorial Park
12 博物馆	12. The University Museum
13 旭日楼(校友之家)	13. Xuri Building (Alumni's Home)
14 师魂石碑	14. The Shihun (Teacher's Soul) Stelae

1 四平路校区正门
The main entrance of the Siping Campus

四平路校门朝向正东,红褐色的圆弧院墙围绕灰白色的校门,圆中寓方,方外有圆,方圆有致,寓意着"为方以矩,为圆以规"。"同济大学"校名由著名书法家舒同题写。

校门始建于 1950 年,采用牌楼门牌样式,表面仿细斩假石处理,门眉浅浮雕,整体庄重而朴素。1997 年采用学生的设计方案进行改造,保留四方门主体,院墙整体后移形成半弧形。新校门形态具有现代感,水平向的门廊将广场与旧校门围合起来;以厚重石材饰面的柱廊与由金属和玻璃构成的休息等候区域相得益彰。与墩实沉稳的旧校门相比,新门廊显得更加轻盈。旧校门彰显同济厚重历史,新门廊寓意同济美好未来。

The main entrance of the Siping Campus faces the east. The square gray gate is surrounded by reddish-brown arc walls, an implicit demonstration of the harmonious coexistence of square and round shapes. It denotes a concept of the Chinese philosophy: nothing can be accomplished without norms or standards, with which square and round shapes are formed. The four Chinese characters of Tongji University were inscribed by a famous Chinese calligrapher SHU Tong.

The main entrance was first built in 1950 after the style of a memorial archway. It was finely polished and crowned with a bas-relief, looking simple and elegant. In 1997, the entrance underwent a transformation based upon a design by students of architecture at Tongji. The square gate was retained and the old enclosing wall was moved backwards to form an arc shape. The modern-looking new entrance has winding corridors along the arc walls, which encircle the old gate and its foreground. The traditional stone arc walls stand in harmony next to the waiting area paved with metal and glass. The winding corridors decorated with stone materials look dynamic and rhythmical in contrast to the thick and solid square gate. As an integral part of Tongji's history, the main entrance keeps the tale of the old days and tells the story of today.

2 毛主席塑像
The Statue of Chairman Mao

走进同济校门,迎面即可看见毛主席的塑像,主席面带微笑,右手高举,向经过的师生和来访者挥手致意。毛主席塑像是同济园的标志性景观之一,每年即将离校的毕业生、南来北往的访客,都会在毛主席像前合影留念。

毛主席塑像于1967年5月开始建造,当年7月1日落成,由晚霞色花岗岩砌成。塑像高7.1米,基座高3米,总高10.1米,这些数字分别暗合着中国共产党生日、三座大山的推翻和中华人民共和国国庆日。二十世纪九十年代塑像修建时,在基座上镶嵌了大字"伟大领袖和导师毛主席永远活在我们心中"。

毛主席塑像由同济师生在没有先例、没有资料可参考的情况下,自行设计、建造,既解决了悬挑、抗震问题,又形态庄重、富有神韵。

Upon entering the main entrance, you will find the Statue of Chairman Mao standing right in front of you as if Chairman Mao is greeting you with a smile and a waving hand. The Statue of Chairman Mao is a landmark at Tongji University. Both students and visitors love to have their pictures taken in front of the Statue.

The construction of the Statue started in May 1967 and completed in July of the same year. The Statue made of granite with the color of sunset glow, is 10.1m tall in total with 7.1m for the figure and 3m for the base. The three numbers, respectively stand for the National Day--1st of Oct, the founding day of the Communist Party of China--1st of July, and the day marking the turnover of the three mountains of imperialism, feudalism and capitalism, which weighed like mountains on the backs of the Chinese people before the establishment of new China. In the 1990s when the Statue was renovated, a line was engraved on the base of the Statue: Our great leader Chairman Mao will live in our hearts forever.

The Statue was designed and built by Tongji teachers and students without any precedential models for reference. They not only solved the technical problems of anti-earthquake as well as overhanging, but also gave a solemn and vividly charming look to the Statue.

3 国立柱
The Memorial Columns

There are two Memorial Columns at Tongji University, Jiwang Column meaning to continue the past cause, and Kailai Column meaning to develop a bright future. They are symmetrically placed in the centers of the southern and northern lawns on the Siping Campus. The tall and solemn-looking columns remind people of the old days of Tongji University.

The Memorial Columns made after the style of the merit-recording stela, are comprised of four parts: a base, a shaft, a head and inscriptions. The head is carved like a budding flower stretching out in all directions. On the flower sits a conical stone plate which holds a bronze crown as the top of the column. The Memorial Columns, with delicate carvings, elegant shapes and rich colors, have enriched the cultural heritage of Tongji. The bronze casting of the former name of the University "National Tongji University" was fixed on the side of the stone plate of each column. The forceful and elegant style of the Chinese characters on the casting was after the stone inscription style of the famous calligrapher YAN Zhenqin in the Tang Dynasty.

"国立同济大学纪念柱"——"继往""开来"柱，庄重挺拔、古朴秀丽，分别矗立在四平路校区校前区南北两片绿地中央，形制一体，对称分布，见证了同济悠久的历史和沧桑的岁月。

纪念柱采用纪功柱的形式，主要由柱础、柱身、柱头、柱铭四部分组成。柱头部分采用意象化的石刻拱形物，四向张开，犹如含苞欲放的花朵，其上托住一块锥台状方石盘，方石盘的上端安置青铜的宝冠作为纪念柱的收头。细腻的雕刻、丰富的造型、深沉浑厚的色泽表现出大方庄重、古朴典雅的文化底蕴。"国立同济大学"的铜铸件，被分别铆固在两块石方盘的不同侧面上，其字体选自唐代著名书法家颜真卿的碑帖，古朴苍劲，端庄挺拔。

4 闻学堂
Haven of Classical Literature

"闻学堂"是在四平路校区图书馆南10楼内独辟的一方雅舍,内部装修古色古香。闻学堂独享460平方米的四方空间,内设演讲报告区、阅览座位以及书画作品、古代机械、茶艺等展示和交流区域,内藏中国传统文化相关书籍5 000余册,是学校重要的中华传统文化传承基地。"闻学堂"集传统文献借阅、展示、研讨三项功能于一体,通过展览、互动、体验并结合传统的阅读、交流、讲座等形式,搭建创新形式的传统文化教育平台,为学生营造出一个传统文化学习与美学熏陶的空间。

The Haven of Classical Literature decorated with traditional Chinese flavor is a graceful room on the 10th floor of the Tongji University Library. In an area of 460m², there is a lecture section, a reading section, communication section for showcasing traditional Chinese paintings, calligraphy and tea art. It has a collection of more than 5,000 books on traditional Chinese culture. As an important base to promote traditional Chinese cultural heritage, Haven of Classical Literature functions as a reading room, an exhibition hall and a conference room. It provides a platform for students to learn traditional Chinese culture and aesthetics through exhibitions, interaction, reading and lectures.

5 校史馆
The University History Gallery

校史馆位于四平路校区东侧,建筑面积 1 395 平方米,地上 3 层,建筑高度 13.76 米,于同济大学百年华诞之际建成并投入使用。校史馆外观整体仿二十世纪三十年代吴淞校区女生宿舍楼修建,缀以活泼时尚的现代元素,正中镶嵌的大片玻璃空间,减轻了仿古带来的沉重感。整栋建筑既复古典雅,又高贵大气,象征着同济大学厚重辉煌的历史与光辉灿烂的未来。馆前矗立"同济天下"柱,为百年校庆之日而立,柱上铭曰:"德贤肇建,济人济事;念我爱我,同济无疆!"

馆内通过近千张历史照片,150 多件实物、模型,系统展现了同济大学百余年来百折不挠、上下求索的光辉历程。同时,馆内借助先进设备和高科技手段,创新展览形式,注重参观者的主动参与和体验。同济校史馆将带您领略学校百年历史,体验同济文化,展望美好未来!

The University History Gallery lies on the east side of the Siping Campus with an area of 1,395m² and a height of 13.76m. The three-storey gallery was built to celebrate Tongji's centennial anniversary. The outlook of the Gallery is an imitation of the girls' dorm on the Wusong Campus in the 1930s with infusion of some lively and fashionable contemporary elements. For instance, the large glass space running from bottom to top in the middle of the building effectively relieves the heaviness brought by the vintage look. This elegant and classical building symbolizes Tongji's profound past and promising prospects. In front of the Gallery stands a column known as "Tongji Tianxia", meaning Tongji has its share of responsibility for the fate of the country. It was erected on Tongji's Centennial Anniversary Day with a Chinese inscription that read "De Xian Zhao Jian, Ji Ren Ji Shi; Nian Wo Ai Wo, Tongji Wu Jiang", which could be roughly interpreted as follows. "Tongji University was established by people of merits. It is committed to serving its country and benefiting its people. It remembers and loves me. Tongji University will stand between heaven and earth forever."

The Gallery intensively displays Tongji's glorious history of persistent pursuit and exploration for over a hundred years, with a collection of thousands of historic pictures, 150 objects and models. Meanwhile, the application of hi-tech facilities and means not only creates new ways of exhibition, but also make it possible for visitors to have hands-on experience. The University History Gallery will guide you through Tongji's history, inform you of Tongji's culture and inspire you to look forward to Tongji's future.

6 国豪园
Guohao Park

国豪园位于图书馆西侧。园中矗立有李国豪塑像,该塑像为半身黑色铜像。塑像面带微笑,面容慈祥、目光深邃。

李国豪塑像落成于同济大学百年校庆前夕,既表达了全体同济人对老校长永远的缅怀和追思,也是对后来人的一种激励。

李国豪(1913—2005),著名科学家、教育家、社会活动家,中国科学院院士,中国工程院院士。曾任同济大学校长、名誉校长。李国豪是同济大学历史上最优秀的代表之一,在同济大学百余年发展史上,发挥的作用和影响长远而深刻,堪称"同济之魂"。他是力挽狂澜的科学大师,世界十大著名结构工程学家之一,在南京长江大桥、宝钢一期工程以及我国大跨度叠合梁斜拉桥建设中功勋卓著;他是治校育人的教育家,在担任同济大学校长期间,他以宏伟的气魄和出色的组织领导,为同济大学的发展作出了重要贡献。2003年,李国豪当选首届"上海市教育功臣"。他还是心怀天下的社会活动家,先后担任了上海市科协第二届主席、上海市第六届政协主席等职务,组织开展了一系列社会工作,为国家的发展、社会的进步付出了大量辛劳和心血。

To the west of the University Library lies Guohao Park where stands a dark bronze bust of Li Guohao. Li's amiable and profound smile was vividly depicted on the statue which was completed for Tongji's centennial anniversary in memory of the late university president and to inspire tomorrow's generations.

Mr. LI Guohao (1913-2005) was a famous scientist, educator, social activist, member of both the Chinese Academy of Sciences and the Chinese Academy of Engineering, president and honorary president of Tongji University. He was one the most outstanding students of Tongji University, who played an important role of profound and lasting significance for over 100 years in the course of development of the university and was referred to as the Soul of Tongji. He was a scientist of vision and one of the Ten Most Famous Structural Engineers in the World. He made remarkable achievements in the construction of Nanjing Yangtze Bridge, Bao Steel Phase One project and the long-span cable-stayed bridges in China. He was a great educator who made remarkable contributions to the development of Tongji University with his wisdom and art of leadership during his time as president of the university. He was awarded Hero Educator of Shanghai in 2003. He was also a social activist who was dedicated to the development of the country and the society and actively organized social activities as the second Chairman of Shanghai Society of Science and Technology and as the Chairman of the Sixth Shanghai Political Consultative Committee.

7 三好坞
Sanhaowu Garden

清波荡漾,垂柳碧影,白鹅戏水,花香浮动……多么浪漫、美好!这一处景致,就是每一位同济人眼前、梦中的三好坞。

三好坞是典型的中国园林式景区,集竹林、假山、径庭、小桥、流水于一体,相映成趣,颇富"曲径幽幽品江南"之意蕴。

三好坞是二十世纪五十年代由师生义务劳动、一铲一锄挖凿兴建而成,取名"三好",寓意"好学好思好辩",也有说得名于毛主席所提倡的"身体好、学习好、工作好"之"三好"。三好坞由著名古建筑学家陈从周先生亲自设计,他将"山林起伏,错落有致"的园林建设原则融入其中,提出了"挖河引流,建设湖心小岛,以两座木桥与外界相连,在岛上堆起高低起伏三座假山"的构想。"三好坞"园名以及"枕流""隐秀"两座桥名也是由他所题。

Rippling limpid water, graceful willow shadows, white geese and pervading aroma of flowers come merrily together to present an extraordinarily romantic and beautiful scene at the Sanhaowu Garden, a dreamland of Tongji University.

Sanhaowu Garden, typical of Chinese gardens, encompasses a bamboo forest, rockeries, a pavilion, a zigzag bridge and water, from which visitors could have a taste of "the southern style of the Yangtze River through the subtle and delicate scenery".

The garden was built by teachers and students with shovels and their bare hands in the 1950s. Its name "Sanhao", literally means "Three Merits", i.e. "excellence in learning, thinking and differentiating". Another interpretation is it was named after Chairman Mao's well-known saying of "keeping healthy, studying hard and working well". The Sanhaowu Garden was designed by a famous landscape designer of Tongji University, CHEN Congzhou who specialized in the construction of classical Chinese gardens. He employed the principle of "intriguing arrangement of mountains and forest" in his design and conceived the idea of "making a river by introducing diversions, building a small island right at the center of the lake, connecting to the outside world with two wooden bridges and creating three rockeries on the island". CHEN who was also known as a calligrapher, inscribed the Chinese characters for the name of the Garden "San Hao Wu" and for the names of the two bridges of "Zhen Liu" and "Yin Xiu" in the Garden, meaning sleeping by water, and hidden beauty respectively.

8 孔园（千秋园）
Kongyuan Garden (Qianqiu Garden)

孔园位于大礼堂南侧，一尊孔子塑像屹立于绿树掩映之中。孔子像四周，绿树如茵，碧草连连，加上入口处的一排白色拱门装饰墙，使整个园区显示出一种别样的风景。

孔园景点于2002年建成，其内的孔子塑像则由孔子的家乡山东省济宁市人民政府为祝贺同济大学95周年校庆而赠送。孔子是中华思想文化的集大成者，儒家学说的创始人，我国古代伟大的思想家、政治家、教育家。他的哲学思想提倡"仁义""礼乐""德治教化"以及"君以民为体"。孔子一生从事教育事业，他广收门徒，相传弟子三千，被后人尊为"万世师表"及"至圣先师"。在孔子像前举办的祭孔仪式表达着同济大学师生对中华优秀传统文化的敬意、尊重和弘扬。

Kongyuan Garden is located in the south of the auditorium, with a statue of Confucius standing amid trees and bushes. The garden is made distinctive by the Confucius statue surrounded by lush trees and green grasses, and by a white arch with a decoration wall at the entrance.

The Garden was built in 2002 with a donation of the Confucius' statue by Confucius' hometown, the Jining Municipal People's Government of Shandong Province to celebrate the 95th anniversary of Tongji University. Confucius was a master of Chinese culture, the founder of Confucianism, a philosopher and an educator in ancient China. He advocated "benevolence", "rituals", "moral education", and "people-centered empirical governance". Confucius devoted his whole life to teaching and was known to have taken as many as 3000 disciples under his guidance. Therefore, he was hailed by his descendants as the Master Teacher for Generations and a Holy Prophet. A ceremony in memory of the Confucius is held each year at Tongji University to strengthen the etiquette education in students and to promote and pay respect to the fine Chinese traditional cultures.

9 爱校路（樱花大道）
Aixiao Road (the Sakura Avenue)

早春时节，樱花盛开，似云似霞，如诗如画。游人如织，比肩接踵，笑语盈盈，倩影盼盼……同济大学"樱花大道"美不胜收，名闻遐迩。

二十世纪九十年代，日本友人赠送给学校百株樱花树苗，学校将其种植于赤峰路校门入口的爱校路两侧，以此见证中日友谊和作为学校发展的美好象征。此后，樱花树苗茁壮成长，日久成荫，繁花盛开时，吸引了校内师生和校外市民前来观赏，爱校路遂另得美名"樱花大道"。

In the early spring of every year, the sakura along the Sakura Avenue of Tongji University is in full bloom like riveting rosy clouds. The avenue is jammed with endless flow of visitors, savoring and photographing the romantic moment with friends and families. In recent years, local people in Shanghai have thronged to the Sakura Avenue of Tongji University to enjoy the fabulous scene of sakura blossoms.

In 1990s, a hundred sakura saplings donated by Japanese friends of the University were planted on both sides of the Aixiao Road near the entrance on Chifeng Road at the Siping Campus to mark the friendship between China and Japan and to symbolize the development of Tongji University. The sakura trees grew fast and well and were in good shape after some years. Since then, when the spring comes, hundreds and thousands of people from both inside and outside the University have flocked to the Aixiao Road for the charming scenery projected by endless clusters of fully-blossomed sakura. Therefore, Aixiao Road has earned itself a nickname as the Sakura Avenue.

10 德文图书馆
German Library

德文图书馆位于中德学部大楼内,面积近 3 000 平方米,内藏德文纸质图书 2.5 万册,为亚洲最大德文图书馆。

在日常图书借阅服务之外,德文图书馆还以访谈、音像、影视、展览等多种形式,面向校内外开展跨文化交流、小型音乐会、主题沙龙、专题讲座、文化教育第二课堂、专题阅读、留学生服务、智库支持服务等各类主题活动。德文图书馆正成为学校以对德交流为特色的国际文化交流中心。

The German Library (Deutschen Bibliothek) is located in the Building of the Sino-German Institute (Chinesisch Deutsche Hoschschule (CDH)) with an area of nearly 3,000m². The library has a collection of 25,000 books in German, the largest of its kind in Asia.

In addition to the routine services of book lending and reading, the German Library is home to many other activities such as cross-cultural communication, chamber concerts, themed salons, lectures and reading, after-class cultural education as well as international student service and think tank support by means of interviews, audio-visual records, films and TV programs, and exhibitions. The German Library has become an international cultural exchange center between Tongji University and its counterparts in Germany.

11 一·二九纪念园
The 1·29 Memorial Park

1948年1月29日,以同济大学学生为首的上海进步青年学生在中国共产党领导下,为了国家的前途命运和人民的根本利益,高举"反迫害、争民主"的旗帜,展开了一场反腐败统治、争取民主权利的伟大斗争,为迎接上海的解放做出了贡献,在上海的中国学生爱国运动史册上留下了光荣的一页,史称"同济大学'一·二九'事件"。为了铭记这一重要事件,当年该事件发生的主要地点——同济大学工学院的礼堂,被命名为"一·二九礼堂"。

为了纪念在"一·二九"事件中受到迫害的爱国学生和革命时期献身的同济英烈,1987年,学校在一·二九礼堂旁修建了一·二九纪念园。整个纪念园采用青石、汉白玉为基色,四周种植青松翠柏,静穆庄严,郁郁葱葱。园内有一条迂回曲折的小溪,溪上铺花岗石路面、桥面,将4个方形园林空间连接起来。该纪念园已成为上海市青少年教育基地,也成为全校师生、全市青少年接受爱国主义教育的重要场所。

On January 29, 1948, students in Shanghai headed by those from Tongji University launched a campaign against corruption under the leadership of the Communist Party of China. To pave the way for the liberation of Shanghai, they fought bravely and devoted their young lives "against persecution and for democracy". They made great contributions to the future of the country and the interests of its people. This patriotic student movement which marked a glorious page in Chinese history was referred to as "the 1·29 Incident of Tongji University". The auditorium of Tongji University's Engineering School, a major site where the incident happened, was named "the 1·29 Auditorium" after this important event.

In memory of the patriotic students persecuted in the "the 1·29 Incident" and killed during the revolutionary period, a Student Movement Memorial Park was built next to the 1·29 Auditorium in 1987. With blue stones and white marbles for its construction base, the park, surrounded by lush pines and cypresses, lies in a quiet and tranquil atmosphere. Inside the park runs a zigzag stream, over which a granite pavement links four square spaces of the park. The Memorial Park has become an Education Base for Teenagers at Shanghai as well as an important place for teachers and students of Tongji University and young people to receive the patriotic education.

12 博物馆
The University Museum

博物馆位于一·二九礼堂西侧的一·二九大楼内,共三层,建筑面积4 430平方米。博物馆改建工程,是中国建筑学会建筑创作银奖作品。整个改建过程中,建筑物的外部形式特征都以修缮的方式得以保留,如人四坡顶屋面、白色粉刷外墙、有分段的连续长窗、简洁的和式风格等。门厅的内侧界面也保留了原建筑外立面的窗洞的格局,两层通高的室间,新旧元素对比分明,交接清晰。

博物馆的一楼、二楼为临展厅,三楼是"中国建筑与建筑文化展示厅"和"中国古代机械复原模型展示厅"两个陈列展厅。在博物馆还有可供参观者休憩的咖啡厅、研讨室、闻道堂(培训教室)和接待室等。自开馆以来,博物馆陆续举办了"长征与遵义会议——纪念红军长征胜利八十周年展览""匠心传承 剑语瓷言——龙泉青瓷宝剑名家作品展""敦煌壁画艺术精品高校公益巡展"等十几个展览,吸引了众多师生及市民前来参观,并受到交口称赞。

一·二九大楼始建于1942年,白墙黑瓦,透明门廊和长廊,既具现代感又蕴涵历史气息。大楼得名于1948年1月29日发生的"反饥饿、反内战"的"一·二九"运动,被列入"上海市优秀历史保护建筑"。

Located inside the 1·29 Building to the west of the 1·29 Auditorium, the University Museum encompasses three storeys with an area of 4,430 m². The renovation project of the museum won a Silver Award issued by the Architectural Society of China (ASC). In the renovation process, the exterior features of the original building were preserved carefully. Such features were spelt out by its four-slope roof facades, its white-painted walls, its long windows with intervals and its overwhelming simple style. The window style in the original building was also retained in the inner side of the hallway with the interweaved old and new elements in a two-story space.

The first and second floors of the museum are for temporary exhibitions. There are two more exhibition halls on the third floor as a Showcase of Chinese Architecture and Architectural Culture and a Showcase of Reduplicated Models of Ancient Chinese Mechanicals. There is also a cafe, a seminar room, Wendao Room (for training) and a reception room available for visitors to the museum. Since its opening to the public, the Museum has held a number of themed exhibitions, such as the Long March and Zunyi Conference -- Commemorating the 80th Anniversary of the Long March, Famous Works of Longquan Celadon Swords and Selected Dunhuang Murals and Art Works which won high praise by teachers, students and visitors from all over the country.

The 1·29 Building was built in 1942. Its white walls, black tiles, transparent porch and promenade, were both modern and historical. The building was named after the 1·29 Movement of Resistance against Hunger and Civil War which broke out in January 29th, 1948. The 1·29 Building is now listed as one of Outstanding Historic Buildings in Shanghai.

13 旭日楼（校友之家）
Xuri Building (Alumni's Home)

旭日楼是一栋位于逸夫楼与中法中心之间、在一片水杉丛林掩映下的二层灰砖小楼，现为"校友之家"，是校友返校礼遇、聚会、讲座、沙龙等的活动场所，也是校内重要接待活动及师生交流活动的场所之一。

一楼设"济济堂"、接待室和会议室。"济济堂"寓意着"同心同德同舟楫，济人济事济天下"的同济情怀，布置有沙发、茶座、书架，供校友师生休闲、交流。接待室和会议室可满足常规会议的需求。二楼设会议室、书房和多功能厅，可满足聚会、演讲、沙龙等不同形式的活动。

旭日楼始建于1947年，2005年复修重建。

The Xuri Building, a two-storey gray brick building amid metasequoia trees between the Yifu Building and the Sino-French Center, is home to Alumni of Tongji University. It serves as a venue to receive the alumni, to have meetings, seminars, salons on the one hand, and as a site for important receptions and communication between teachers and students on the other hand.

The first floor consists of Jiji Hall, a reception room and a conference room. The Jiji Hall implies the Tongji spirit of doing things "with one heart, with one dream and with the same future, for the people, for the whole world and for the same planet". There are sofas, tea stands and book shelves available to the alumni, teachers and students in the Jiji Hall. The reception room and the conference room are available for most meetings. The conference rooms, study rooms, and multi-function rooms on the second floor are often used for such activities as parties, speeches and salons.

The Xuri Building was built in 1947 and was renovated in 2005.

14 师魂石碑
The Shihun (Teacher's Soul) Stelae

在教学南楼东侧,有一组称为"师魂"的纪念碑,以纪念原同济大学附中叶懋英老师忠诚党的事业、一生教书育人的崇高师德。叶懋英曾任职于同济大学工农速成中学,先后任工农预科主任、附中校长,是上海市首批特级教师。

三座石碑分别刻有叶老师的生平事迹、陈从周先生题写的"师魂"大字以及"捧着一颗心来,不带半根草去"的朴实话语。

On the east side of the South Teaching Building, there are a group of stelae named "Shihun" meaning teacher's soul. The stelae were built in memory of Ms. YE Maoying, a teacher from the High School Affiliated to Tongji University, who devoted her life to the great cause of education. Ms. YE taught at the former Middle School for Workers and Peasants of Tongji University, and acted as the director of the Preparatory Course for Workers and Peasants and the principal of the High School Affiliated to Tongji University. She was awarded as one of the first Shanghai Master Teachers.

The three stelae are engraved respectively with an introduction of Ms.YE, an inscription of the Chinese characters "Shi Hun" by CHEN Congzhou, a famous calligrapher in China, and a quote from YE, "teaching with a sincere heart without asking for any return".

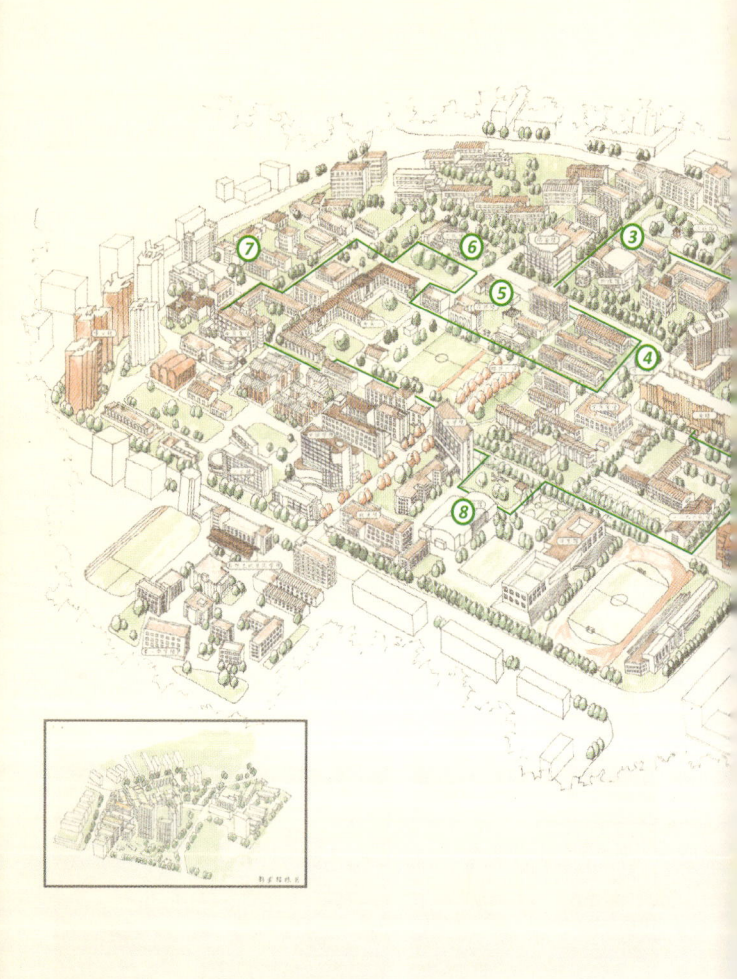

绿色之路 (节能类)
The Green Path
Buildings of Energy Conservation

- 1 行政楼
- 2 文远楼
- 3 运筹楼
- 4 人工湿地
- 5 学生浴室
- 6 大礼堂
- 7 环境科学与工程学院实验楼
- 8 游泳馆
- 9 中法中心
- 10 上海国际设计一场

- 1. The Administration Building
- 2. Wenyuan Building
- 3. Yunchou Building
- 4. The Artificial Wetland
- 5. The Student Shower House
- 6. The Auditorium
- 7. Environmental Engineering Center
- 8. The Swimming Pool
- 9. Sino-French Center
- 10. Shanghai International Design Center

1 行政楼
The Administration Building

行政楼位于四平路校门北侧,南北两栋各5层,外型呈阶梯型,内有走廊相连。2006年,行政楼外立面进行绿化改建,引入高技轻钢、植物立面的生态建筑方式,通过立面藤蔓植物枝叶冬夏季节的疏密变化起到对建筑物保温与隔热的作用,同时植物攀爬面遮盖了空调外机,大大美化了行政楼外观。绿化改建后的行政楼外墙上疏密有致、常年青翠的一条条绿色"瀑布"自上而下垂落,藤蔓上兼有数朵当季鲜花盛开,赏心悦目,增添了无限生机和活力。

The Administration Building of Tongji University is located on the north side of a square by the main entrance of the Siping Campus. It encompasses two five-storey buildings both on the north and south. The two buildings are shaped in the style of staircases from outside, and are connected with corridors from inside. In 2006, the facade of the Administration Building was renovated for environmental purposes where ecological construction methods were adopted for the application of high-tech light steel and plant-based walls. Therefore, the automatic insulation effects of the facades can be achieved through change of the plant density all year around. Meanwhile, the engines of air conditioners hanging on the walls are covered by the climbing plants so that the Administration Building looks neat and pleasing without showing any electric devices. The facades of the newly renovated administration building, with verdant plants evenly distributed on the walls and a plant-made "Green Waterfall" drooping from the rooftop, present a feast to the eyes of passers-by, especially when they are dotted with some seasonal flowers.

2 文远楼
Wenyuan Building

2005年文远楼进行了节能改造,其中使用了包括地源热泵技术、太阳能燃气补能系统、冷吊顶技术在内的十余项节能技术,节能60%~70%。文远楼是上海首座改造为生态建筑的历史保护建筑。

The Wenyuan Building of Tongji University was renovated in 2005 with application of more than 10 energy-efficient technologies, including geothermal heat pump technology, solar gas refueling system and cold ceiling technology, which saved 60% -70% of energy. The building was the first historical building in Shanghai that was turned ecological.

3 运筹楼
Yunchou Building

运筹楼,始建于 1983 年,建筑面积 4 127 平方米。"运筹"二字,典出《史记》,原意指谋兵布阵。运筹楼原为同济大学经济与管理学院大楼,意为统筹规划、优化决策。2014 年,意大利环境、领土与海洋部、中国科学技术部与同济大学三方联合开展绿色改建工作。改建过程中,采用多项节能措施:优化供水系统;使用多联机式空调系统,节能降耗,节省空间;采用高效照明及照明控制系统,对办公室、教室照明分组分区控制,对公共场所(走廊、门厅)采用分组分区集中控制;利用可再生能源,屋面设置光伏板,将太阳能电量直接利用到建筑耗电量中;采用节水器具;屋顶进行绿化并使用绿色建材。

改建后的运筹楼于建校 110 周年之际修葺落成。改建之后,旧词新解,意为筹谋帷幄之中,决胜千里之外,胸怀中华,放眼寰宇,共图全球可持续发展。

Yunchou Building, built in 1983, covers an area of 4,127m². The two Chinese characters for the name "Yun" and "Chou" were from the Chinese classical *Records of the Grand Historian*, originally meaning the strategy of commanding military troops. The building was for the School of Economics and Management of Tongji University, where people were taught to make balanced plans and optimized decisions. In 2014, the building underwent green renovation with joint support by the Italian Ministry of Environment, Land and Sea (IMELS), the Ministry of Science and Technology of China and Tongji University. In the renovation process, a number of energy-saving measures were adopted including optimized water supply system, multi-connected air-conditioning system, efficient energy and space use; efficient lighting and lighting control system for grouped lighting control over offices and classrooms and centralized lighting control over public places like corridors and lobbies; use of renewable energy with installment of photovoltaic panels on the roof, which transformed the solar power directly into the power consumption of the building; employment of water-saving appliances and plant-based roof in addition to use of environmentally friendly construction materials.

The renovation of the building was completed just before the 110th anniversary of Tongji University. Since then, a new interpretation has been attached to Yunchou Building, i.e. plotting strategies here and win victories a thousand miles away. By extension, it means to work together to achieve sustainable development of the world by thinking globally though based in China.

4 人工湿地
The Artificial Wetland

学校在同心河旁边建立了大片湿地,地面下铺设吸附性填料,上面加泥土,种上绿色植物。对污水进行过滤净化,从而保证资源的持续利用。人工湿地是一种有效、低成本、环境优化的污水处理装置,它可以通过各种物理、化学以及生物的机制来去除污水中的有机物以及氮磷。

A large area of wetland has been established by the Tongxin River side of the Siping Campus, with absorbent materials laid under the surface. Earth was placed on the top of the surface where green plants were planted. The sewage was treated and purified for sustainable use of resources. The artificial wetland acts as an efficient, low-cost and environmental-friendly device for depriving the sewage of organic materials, nitrogen and phosphorus through physical, chemical, and biological mechanisms.

5 学生浴室
The Student Shower House

学生浴室采用太阳能智能集中供热系统,通过太阳能集热模块吸收太阳能,对管道内的冷水加温。同时采用"中水回用"系统,利用膜生物反应器组合工艺进行污水处理,将处理之后的水直接用于景观及绿化灌溉。还增设了热交换池,充分利用洗浴废水的剩余热能加热新鲜水,节能超过30%。

A solar energy central heating system is employed in the Student Shower House, which absorbs the solar energy through a Solar Heat Collection Module before heating the cold water in the pipeline. Meanwhile, the "Reclaimed Water Reuse" system was used for sewage treatment through a combination of membrane bioreactors which send treated water directly to the landscape for irrigation. Moreover, there is a heat exchange pool for heating the fresh water by reusing the residual heat from waste water, which may save over 30% of energy.

6 大礼堂
The Auditorium

大礼堂于2005年进行了保护性修缮改造。在改造过程中,多种节能措施得到应用,如采用高效风冷热泵机组和数码变频热泵机组组成的冷热源、自然通风和过渡季节全新风供冷及地道风预冷(热)、座椅柱脚下送风等,大大节省了能源。

The Auditorium was renovated in 2005 for protective purposes. In the renovation process, various energy efficient measures were adopted. For instance, the cold and heat sources were created respectively by high-efficiency air-cooled heat pump units and digital variable frequency heat pump units. In addition, natural ventilation, fresh cold wind supply in transitional seasons, pre-cooling/heating of tunnel wind, and wind supply from under the chairs also help save energy in an efficient way.

7 环境科学与工程学院实验楼
Environmental Engineering Center

环境科学与工程学院实验楼在生态建筑设计、自然通风、可再生资源利用、绿色环保材料、室内环境技术、绿色配置技术等方面体现出节能环保特点。

通风方面采用双层皮幕墙，保证通风量，利用楼梯间的烟囱效应加强自然通风，增强建筑通风效果。建筑南立面采用水平遮阳百叶，调整百叶角度增加采光，屋顶玻璃采光顶搭遮阳棚。屋面配合地毯式屋顶绿化，种植草皮和地被植物，西晒严重的山墙种植垂直绿化植物，屋顶安装光伏方阵。同时，利用被动式太阳能技术增强采光和遮阳功能。

The Environmental Engineering Center is unique in its ecological architecture design, natural ventilation, use of renewable construction materials, indoor environmental technologies, and green distribution technologies.

The Double-Skin Facade (DSF) has been adopted in the Environmental Engineering Center to ensure best ventilation. Chimney efficiency in staircases is utilized to help increase natural ventilation. The southern facade of the building is equipped with horizontal blinds, whose angles can be adjusted to increase the lighting. Sun shades are set up for the glass skylight system on the roof of the building. Rooftops are covered with turfs and plants, and vertical plants hang on the west wall of the building which suffers most from sunshine at sunset, and photovoltaic (PV) arrays have been installed on the roof of the building. Meanwhile, the use of passive solar technology can enhance the lighting and sun-shade effects.

8 游泳馆
The Swimming Pool

同济大学游泳馆于2007年竣工,为钢结构屋盖。建筑采用可开启屋顶技术,主体部分屋盖固定部分采用梭形张弦梁结构,活动部分采用单层加劲桁架结构体系。游泳馆的生态和节能技术措施主要体现在屋顶开启技术、太阳能集热技术以及空气源热泵技术等方面。

The Swimming Pool of Tongji University was completed in 2007. A retractable roof technology was employed for the steel structure roof in the construction of the building. A String Beam Structure (SBS) was used for the main body and the fixed part of the roof, and a single-layer stiffened truss structure for the retractable part. The use of ecological and energy-saving technologies for the Swimming Pool are showcased by the retractable roof, the solar heat collection and the air source heat pump.

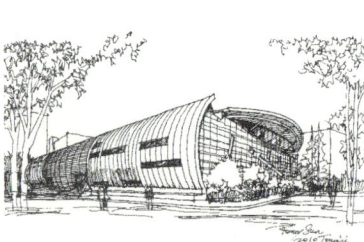

9 中法中心
Sino-French Center

中法中心在建造过程中采用地下温室顶部自然采光、外墙材料选择耐候钢板和水泥纤维板等节能措施。耐候钢,即耐大气腐蚀钢,是介于普通钢和不锈钢之间的低合金钢系列,耐候钢由普碳钢添加少量铜、镍等耐腐蚀元素而成,具有优质钢的强韧、塑延、抗疲劳等特性。同时,它具有耐锈,使构件抗腐蚀延寿、减薄降耗,省工节能等特点。主要用于铁道、车辆、桥梁、塔架等长期暴露在大气中使用的钢结构。

Natural Lighting was used for the top of the underground greenhouse, and weathering steel plates and cement-based fiber boards for the facades during construction of the Sino-French Center. Weathering steel known as steel resistant to corrosion of air is a low-alloy steel between ordinary steel and stainless steel. The weathering steel is made of carbon steel with a small number of corrosion-resistant elements, such as copper and nickel. It is characterized by such properties as being highly resilient, malleable and fatigue-proof. At the same time, it exhibits resistance to rust, enables other components to become more rust-resistant and durable, thus helping save labor and energy. It is now widely used for steel structures such as railways, vehicles, bridges and towers under long exposure to air.

10 上海国际设计一场
Shanghai International Design Center

上海国际设计一场由原巴士一汽停车库改建而成,是环同济知识圈的组成部分。项目采用建筑光伏一体化系统,为2009年财政部、建设部的光电建筑示范项目。

在节能方面,该建筑为既有建筑改造项目,避免了巨大建筑拆除时钢筋混凝土垃圾的产生,节约混凝土方量约25 000立方米,相当于减少二氧化碳排放12 000吨。另外,采用屋面晶体硅组件、薄膜太阳电池组件共5 200多平方米,在二、三层和五层采用光伏遮阳板和硅基薄膜建筑光伏一体化组件。同时采用中水回用节能措施。

Shanghai International Design Center grew out of the bus garage of the former First Automobile Work (FAW). The center, as a part of the Knowledge Economy Circle around Tongji University, is equipped with an integrated photovoltaic system. It is a demonstration project of the Building Integrated Photovoltaic Programs launched jointly by the Ministry of Finance and the Ministry of Construction in 2009.

The transformation of the building was an energy saving project, for 25,000m³ waste of concrete was avoided as a result of demolishing old building, which was equivalent to a reduction of 12,000 tons of carbon dioxide emission. In addition, more than 5,200m² of crystalline silicon and thin-film solar modules were used in the renovation of the building, with the second, third and fifth floors respectively installed with the photovoltaic sun shades and silicon-based Building Integrated Photovoltaic (BIPV) components. Meanwhile, reclaimed water was also reused in the transformation.

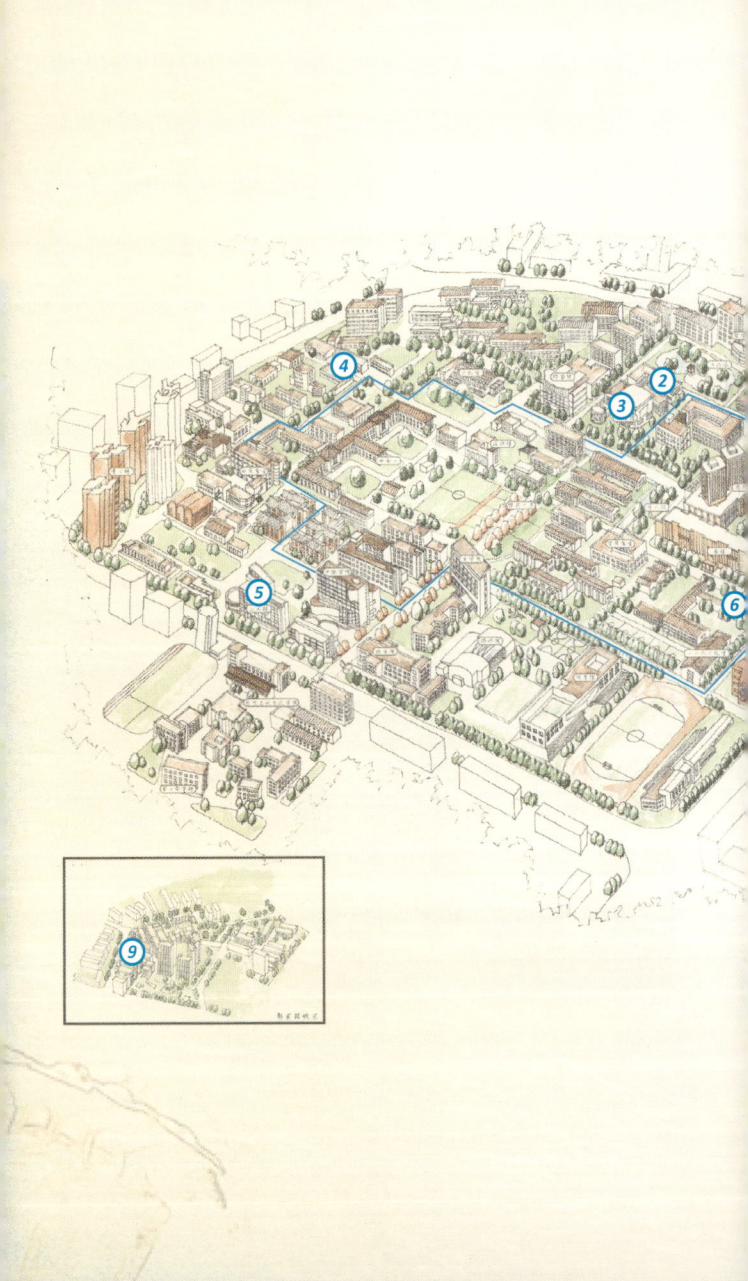

蓝色之路（科技类）
The Blue Path
Buildings of Science and Technology

○ 1 建筑与城市规划学院
    艺术造型实验室
  2 声学馆
  3 物理实践工作站
  4 结构试验中心
  5 土木工程教学
    创新实践基地
  6 同济创业谷
  7 深海探索馆
  8 同济大学 Fablab
  9 微小飞机实验室

○ 1. The Innovation Laboratory of College of Architectural Design and Urban Planning

2. The Institute of Acoustics

3. The Physical Experiment Workstation

4. The Structure Testing Center

5. The Civil Engineering Innovation Teaching Base

6. Venture Valley of Tongji University

7. The Deep Sea Exploration Gallery

8. The Creative Workshop of College of Design and Innovation

9. The Simulation Plane Workstation

1 建筑与城市规划学院艺术造型实验室
The Innovation Laboratory of College of Architectural Design and Urban Planning

艺术造型实验室设于建筑与城市规划学院 D 楼一楼，面积约 800 平方米，展示由学生们创作的丰富多彩、形态各异并充满想像力、创造力的艺术作品：用细木条精巧搭建的意大利佛罗伦萨百花大教堂结构模型、2010 世博会中国馆结构模型、古朴而又现代的各种砖雕与木雕作品、色彩绚丽的琉璃作品、精致多变而又不失动感的剪纸作品以及各种编织造型作品。

有兴趣者，还可以亲自动手体验中国传统的拓片制作工艺，并可保留自己的作品。

The Innovation Laboratory is located on the first floor of the Building D of College of Architectural Design and Urban Planning, covering an area of about 800m². Colorful and creative art works made by students are on display here, including an architectural model of the Basilica Di Santa Maria del Fiore in Florence made of fine sticks, a model structure of the China Pavilion of the World Expo 2010, modern brick and wood carvings with ancient glamour, colorful glass works, exquisite and vivid paper-cut works and many other woven art works.

It also allows those who are interested in the traditional Chinese rubbing to sample the production process of artistic creation and make their own products.

2 声学馆
The Institute of Acoustics

物理科学与工程学院声学馆与"三好坞"景观一路之隔。

同济大学声学研究始于二十世纪五十年代中期,目前声学所研究方向包括纳米声成像、医学超声、无损检测、厅堂声学设计、减震降噪、听觉感知等方面。馆内拥有全消声室、混响室、隔声室、驻波馆、消声水池、原子力声显微镜、光纤声传感系统等大型实验设施与设备。其中,混响室、隔声室分别建于1956年、1957年,是国内首建亦是当时国内最大的同类设施。

The Institute of Acoustics, School of Physical Science and Engineering stands opposite the Sanhaowu Garden. Tongji University started its acoustic research in the mid-1950s. At present, its research dimensions range from nano-acoustic imaging, medical ultrasound, non-destructive testing, acoustic design of buildings, vibration absorption and noise reduction to auditory perception. There is an anechoic room, a reverberation room, a soundproof room, a standing wave hall, an anechoic pool, and other experimental facilities, such as the atomic force acoustic microscope (AFAM) and the optical fiber sensing system in the institute. Among them, the reverberation room and the soundproof room were built respectively in 1956 and 1957, the first and the largest of its kind in China at that time.

3 物理实践工作站
The Physical Experiment Workstation

物理实践工作站成立于2007年,为上海市青少年科技人才培养基地之一。科普工作主要包括:物理演示(探索)实验室参观接待活动;各类动手小实验科普活动、科普讲座;中学生物理类研究型学习课题、中学生物理类应用型创新课题指导。

物理演示(探索)实验室常年对外开放,包括力学探索室、振动与波探索室、电磁学探索室、光学探索室、热学探索室、近代物理探索室。参观者在演示实验室教师的指导下可自行动手操作实验仪器,探索物理现象背后的奥秘。

The Physical Experiment Workstation of Tongji University was established in 2007 and has served as one of the Shanghai Training Bases for Young Science and Technology Talents since then. To promote popular science, physical experiments are demonstrated, and hands-on experiments and presentations are organized at the workstation. Help from teachers at Tongji are available to middle school students who are on research programs both in physics and applied physics.

Visitors are welcome to the Physical Demonstration Laboratories at the workstation all year round, which include a mechanical exploration lab, a vibration and wave exploration lab, an electromagnetic exploration lab, an optical exploration lab, a thermal exploration lab and a modern physics exploration lab. Under the guidance of teachers from the workstation, visitors can do experiments with their own hands to explore the mystery of physics.

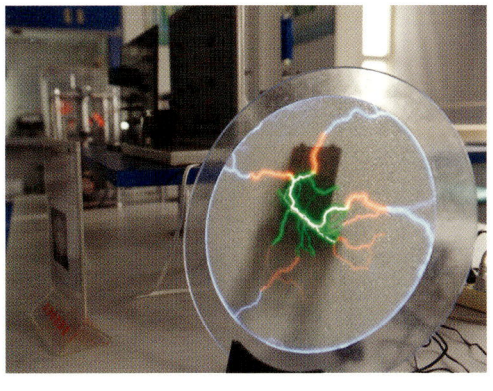

4 结构试验中心
The Structure Testing Center

土木工程学院结构试验中心位于四平路校区西北隅,该中心的教学科研活动始于 1955 年,是国内最早从事建筑结构试验教学科研的单位之一。

目前,结构试验中心拥有三向六自由度模拟地震振动台、1 000kN 电液伺服加载系统、5 000kN 疲劳试验机、大型反力墙和反力台座等一系列大型结构试验设施。其中,三向六自由度模拟地震振动台建于 1983 年,是国内最早引进建设的高性能地震模拟系统。其尺寸 4m×4m,可在负载 25 吨试件时,实现 0.5~100Hz,0~1.2g 多向加载。在该振动台试验的项目包括上海中心、东方明珠广播电视塔、LG 北京大厦、重庆来福士广场等大量超限高层建筑,也涵盖减隔震、控制、摇摆以及自复位等的教学与科研实践项目,试验运行效率位于同行前列。

该中心根据实际比例搭建的结构试验模型与大礼堂遥相呼应,成为校园内颇具特色的景观。

The Structure Testing Center of the College of Civil Engineering is located in the northwestern corner of the Siping campus. The center put to operation in 1955, was one of the first of its kind in China for teaching and research of structure testing.

At present, the center encompasses a series of large-scale facilities for structural testing, such as a three-dimensional Six-DOF Seismic Simulating Shaking Table, a 1,000kN Electro-Hydraulic Loading Servo System, a 5,000kN Fatigue Test Machine and large-scale reaction walls and reaction pedestals. Among them, the Simulating Shaking Table built in 1983, was the first high-performance seismic simulation system introduced to China from abroad. With a size of 4m×4m, it is capable of performing 0.5~ 100Hz and 0~1.2g multi-directional operation with a load of 25 tons. Projects tested on the shaking table included a large number of high-rise buildings beyond code specifications such as the Shanghai Tower, the Oriental Pearl Radio & TV Tower, the LG Twin Towers and Chongqing Raffles City. Other teaching and research projects on seismic response reduction, control, swing, and self-reset are also tested at the shaking table. The center is among the best in China in its operation efficiency.

In front of the center, the structure models of those high-rise buildings made by the Center for testing project an imposingly unique scene against the background of the University Auditorium nearby.

5 土木工程教学创新实践基地
The Civil Engineering Innovation Teaching Base

土木工程教学创新实践基地位于土木工程学院地下一层,成立于2003年9月,总面积约800平方米。

土木工程教学创新实践基地作为国际、国内各种大型结构大赛的主要举办场地,里面陈列着学生在大赛中制作的各式各样的模型:有竹材结合3D打印节点、能行驶负重小车的桥梁,有使用纸张作为原材料、拼接组合、承受冲击荷载的三层楼房,有桐木制成、承受人体重量的高跷,还有精巧细致的抗震仿古楼阁。经过创新实践基地的培训,从这里走出去的学生在国内乃至国际结构大赛中频获奖项,如全美土木工程大赛、全国大学生结构设计大赛等。

在创新实践基地,同学们可以亲自动手制作模型,并加载测试模型的各项性能。

Built in September 2003, the Civil Engineering Innovation Teaching Base is located in the basement of the College of Civil Engineering with an area of about 800m².

It is committed to hosting large-scale domestic and international structure design contests. On display are the works of students from the contests, including 3D printing nodes made of bamboo, a bridge with a loaded car that is driving on it, an assembled three-story building under impact loading made of paper, the stilts made of Paulownia that bear the weight of a human body, exquisite and delicate seismic pavilions. After receiving training at the innovation teaching base, more and more students won awards at domestic and international structure design contests, such as the US Civil Engineering Competition and the National College Students Structure Design Competition.

Students can design and make models with their own hands, and test the performances of the models with various loads at the base.

6 同济创业谷
Venture Valley of Tongji University

同济创业谷致力于弥补大学创新创业链条缺失环节,打通从大学校区到科技园区"最后一公里",建设大学生喜爱的"创业乐园"。

同济创业谷以"催生好的创新创业项目、培育好的创新创业人才、提供好的创新创业服务"为目标,通过硬件支持和软件服务,促进学校、社会、政府、企业、资本五个主体有效互动。创新实验室、宽松创意工作坊、信息咨询中心、微型秀场、宽容便利的外部空间为创新项目提供硬件、空间支持,所有的办公场地、实验室、设备都可以免费使用,还有工商、税务、法律、地方政策等免费咨询……同时发挥教师专业知识、政府优惠政策、社会风投基金等资源,开办"创业谷学堂",推出具有同济特色的创新创业课程包,成立"同济创客联盟"等,营造有利于创新创业的生态环境、倡导创新创业的生活方式,帮助大学生实现创业梦想。

Venture Valley of Tongji University is committed to building the link between academic study and start-up business by serving as "the last leg" from the campus to the science park and creating a Land for Start-up Business for college students.

Aimed at "cultivating innovative start-up projects, developing innovative pioneering talents and providing good service for innovation and entrepreneurship", Venture Valley of Tongji University promotes the interaction among universities, the society, government, industry and the capital through its hardware support and software services. The support and services are available through innovative laboratories, creative workshops, information center, mini-shows and convenient external space. Office space, laboratories and facilities are all available to students at no cost. There is also free consultation service on business, taxation, law and local policies. Venture Valley of Tongji University has already initiated a program known as School of Venture Valley, designed an innovation and entrepreneurship course with Tongji characteristics, and established a Tongji Alliance for Business Starters by making good use of its resources including teachers, favorable government policies and venture investments from the society. It is on its way to creating an ecological environment rooted in a life style of innovation and entrepreneurship for an increasing number of students to realize their entrepreneurial dreams.

7 深海探索馆
The Deep Sea Exploration Gallery

"深海探索馆"展示空间近500平方米,包含"海洋纵览""深海探索""深海遨游""海底观测"四部分内容,以大量声光电等现代化展示技术,赋予各展项生动性和趣味性,形象、直观、立体化呈现了深海迷人的世界,带给参观者全新的多感互动体验。参观者不仅能欣赏到"黑烟囱"喷出的海底热液幻影、活跃在幽暗深海的大量珍奇生物、多姿多彩的海洋微体生物群等深海奇观;还能了解人类探索深海的进程以及深海最新科技与发现,观看《深潜的梦想》《探访深海》《蛟龙号载人深潜器》等多部短片。此外,参观者还能当一回深潜科学家,模拟在"蛟龙号"抓取深海样品,体验深海遨游的神奇。

"深海探索馆"于2014年11月正式开馆,为国内首个以深海为主题的科普陈列馆。该馆属于同济大学深海科普馆二期工程。早在2008年,海洋与地球科学学院就在海洋楼一楼,建成国内首个以深海为主题的科普陈列馆,该馆已成为上海市科普教育基地。

The Deep Sea Exploration Gallery of nearly 500m² has four parts of Ocean Overview, Deep Sea Exploration, Deep Sea Travel and Sea Bottom Observation. The dynamic and fascinating world of deep sea is brought into the view of visitors with the help of acoustic, optical and electrical technologies. Visitors can not only observe the submarine hydrothermal vents emanating from the Black Chimney, a large number of rare marine creatures living in dark deep sea and colorful marine micro-biota clusters, but also learn facts about the progress of human exploration of the deep sea and the latest technology development and discoveries in the deep sea. They also have access to short films, such as the *Deep Dive Dream*, *Visit to the Deep Sea* and *Manned Deep-sea Submersible Jiaolong*. In addition, visitors have a chance of playing the role of scientists and experiencing the wonder of deep-sea travel by catching deep-sea samples from a simulated Jiaolong Deep-sea Submersible.

The Deep Sea Exploration Gallery was open to the public in November 2014. As the first popular science gallery with a theme on the deep ocean in China, it was the continuation of the project of Deep Sea Popular Science Gallery of Tongji University. Back in 2008, the first popular science exhibition hall in China focused on the theme of the deep sea was set up on the first floor of the School of Ocean and Earth Sciences. The exhibition hall has become a Popular Science Education Bases of Shanghai over the years.

8 同济大学 Fablab
The Creative Workshop of College of Design and Innovation

2013年，同济大学设计创意学院创立了中国第一个Fablab实验室(创意工坊)——一个几乎可以制造任何产品和工具的小型工厂。2014年7月，同济大学Fablab首次进入国际Fablab社区，完成了国际认证。

实验室先后举办了跨学科的开放夜、软硬件工作坊等系列活动，承办了教育部中美青年创客大赛、中日韩智能可穿戴大赛、可穿戴暑期学校，开创毕业设计创业项目，孵化了10多个科技硬件类产品。实验室自成立以来，在中国推进开放设计和创新制造方面所取得的丰硕成果，受到了全世界重要实验室的关注和赞赏，在中国乃至全球的创客界声名显赫。

In 2013, the College of Design and Innovation of Tongji University established the first Fablab (Creative Workshop) in China, a small factory that could produce almost any products and tools. In July 2014,the Fablab joined the international community of Fablab for the first time and has become internationally recognized since.

Fablab organized a series of interdisciplinary activities, such as open nights, and hardware and software workshops. Authorized by the Ministry of Education, China, it hosted the Sino-US Young Entrepreneur Competition, China-Japan-South Korea Smart Wearable Competition and the Wearable Summer School. In addition, it initiated the Graduation Design Start-up Projects and developed over 10 hi-tech hardware products. Since the establishment of Fablab, remarkable achievements have been made in promoting open design and innovating manufacturing in China, which has attracted the attention of leading laboratories worldwide and gained a reputation in the start-up business community in the world.

9 微小飞机实验室
The Simulation Plane Workstation

同济大学微小飞机实验室位于彰武路校区航空航天与力学学院,创建于2012年。实验室设有展厅及设计间、制作间、发动机测试设备间。展厅里摆放着由学生自己动手制作的琳琅满目的各种飞机模型:翼展3.5米的无人机样机、2米多高的巨大"飞人"机、世界上最大的电动遥控动力纸飞机、仿1 500年前的古玛雅"黄金飞机"、形态可掬的十二生肖卡通飞机、短距离弹射伞降回收飞机、参照上亿年前翼龙形态制作的仿生飞机等。

参观者在了解飞机制作原理的同时,还可动手参与制作简单的飞机模型。